Original title:

Mellow Tones Inside the Faerie Clay

Copyright © 2025 Swan Charm

All rights reserved.

Author: Eliora Lumiste

ISBN HARDBACK: 978-1-80562-683-1

ISBN PAPERBACK: 978-1-80564-204-6

Shadows Dancing in the Softest Light

In twilight's embrace, where whispers play,
The shadows stretch, then waltz away.
With every flicker, a tale's unfold,
Of secrets long kept and dreams retold.

The moon's soft glow wraps all in silk,
As night unfolds its gentle quilt.
Stars peek through, their laughter bright,
While shadows dance in dreamy flight.

In corners dark, where echoes sleep,
The night descends, its promise deep.
With every breath, the magic grows,
As time drifts softly, like falling snow.

A breeze carries stories, old and wise,
Where silvery clouds weave through the skies.
The heart awakens with a quiet sigh,
In the arms of the night, we learn to fly.

So let your spirit take its chance,
And join the shadows in their dance.
For in this light, your soul will find,
The endless wonder of the mind.

Caresses of the Ethereal Veil

In whispers soft, the night descends,
A tapestry where twilight bends,
Stars like diamonds, dance and sway,
Cradling dreams, they gently play.

Moonbeams weave through shadows deep,
Where ancient secrets softly creep,
Holding time within their arms,
Enchanted by their subtle charms.

A feathered touch, the breeze unfolds,
The stories of the brave retold,
Embracing all, both far and near,
Each caress dissolves the fear.

Through veils of mist, a path is traced,
Where fantasies and thoughts interlaced,
In every sigh, a spark of light,
Guiding hearts through endless night.

Reveries in the Twilight Ember

Amidst the glow of fading day,
The twilight ember starts to play,
A symphony of soft delight,
That paints the stars upon the night.

In every moment, dreams ignite,
Illuminating souls in flight,
With whispering winds that call our name,
We soar on wings, forever untame.

Beneath the arch of twilight's grace,
We find our dreams in time and space,
A tranquil dance, pure magic spun,
Two hearts aligned, forever one.

Each fleeting glance, a story shared,
A bond so deep, eternally bared,
In reveries that softly glow,
Together, through the night we flow.

Serenade of the Dreamweaver's Breath

A lullaby on silver threads,
The dreamweaver gently spreads,
In every note, a world awakes,
Enchanting hearts till morning breaks.

Underneath the starry cloak,
A symphony of dreams bespoke,
With echoes soft in twilight's sway,
We chase the dawn, we dance, we play.

In the stillness, whispers rise,
A serenade beneath the skies,
With each sweet breath of autumn's chill,
We wake the heart, we bend the will.

Through winding paths of starlit streams,
We wander lost within our dreams,
The dreamweaver's touch, a perfect guide,
As we embrace the night, our pride.

Echoed Lullabies of the Enchanted Grove

In an enchanted grove we weave,
Echoes of dreams that we believe,
Where whispers kiss the ancient trees,
And time drifts down upon the breeze.

With every rustle, tales unfold,
Of hearts entwined and spirits bold,
In shadows soft, our hopes ignite,
As lullabies cradle us at night.

The moonlight spills like molten gold,
A tapestry of dreams retold,
With every star, a wish is spun,
In this grove that shelters one.

Here, the night is gently swayed,
In melodies, our fears are laid,
A sanctuary dressed in hues,
Of whispered ventures, we can't refuse.

Tapestry of Sprite and Soil

In fields where wild daisies dance and sway,
The sprites weave magic by night and day.
Beneath the oak, their laughter rings so clear,
Entwined with soil, they gather, drawing near.

With threads of starlight and sunlit beams,
They stitch together our forgotten dreams.
In vibrant hues of emerald and gold,
A story of earth and wonder unfolds.

Each morning dew a whispered tale of grace,
A tapestry spun in this sacred space.
With every breeze, a rustling symphony,
Nature's artistry, wild and free.

The blossoms twirl in harmony, so bright,
In their embrace, darkness yields to light.
The sprites, they flutter, with nimble delight,
Weaving the day, embracing the night.

In this enchanted glade, they reign supreme,
A playful chorus, lost in the dream.
The world, a canvas, painted by their hands,
In every stitch, the magic expands.

Elegy of the Wandering Wisps

Through moonlit woods where shadows loom and sway,
The wisps drift softly, stealing breath away.
They roam the night with secrets held so tight,
In echoing silence, they claim their flight.

With glimmers fading like a distant star,
They beckon souls who wander from afar.
In whispers soft as silken threads they weave,
An elegy of dreams that none believe.

With gentle light, they dance on forest's edge,
A fleeting glimpse, a fragile, trembling pledge.
Yet in their glow, the heart begins to pine,
A beckoning warmth, a whisper divine.

They mourn the mingled paths that once were tread,
Yet through the dark, they guide the lost, the dead.
In silvered whispers, secrets come alive,
For those who listen, hope begins to thrive.

So take your candle, let it burn so bright,
And join the wisps to revel in the night.
For in each flicker lies a story told,
An elegy of wandering souls so bold.

A Symphony of Softened Whispers

In twilight's cradle, where the shadows blend,
A symphony of whispers, dusk to send.
Each note a breath, a sigh from unseen lips,
As night unveils its tapestry of slips.

The breeze it carries tales of those before,
Of love and loss, of dreams upon the shore.
In gentle currents, old memories wake,
A dance of longing, hearts begin to ache.

Amid the fading light, they weave and twine,
Softened whispers like the finest wine.
Each echo glimmers with a sweet embrace,
In every corner, a familiar face.

They whisper secrets of the stars above,
Of fleeting moments wrapped in tender love.
With every flicker, hope is gently stirred,
In this serene hush, no need for words.

So pause and listen to the night unfold,
A symphony of whispers, soft and bold.
Let them wrap 'round you like a velvet shroud,
And in their solace, let your heart feel proud.

Chants from the Hidden Hollow

In the hidden hollow where the shadows lie,
The trees are cloaked in whispers, none ask why.
With mossy stones and whispers soft as lace,
Ancient chants echo through this secret place.

At dusk when fireflies sprinkle the gloom,
Voices of the forest weave tales of bloom.
Forgotten stories linger in the air,
Beckoning those who wander, unaware.

The brooklet babbles secrets old as time,
Each ripple carrying a whispered rhyme.
In unity, the creatures rise and sing,
In this hidden hollow, magic takes wing.

As moonbeams glisten on the silver leaves,
A symphony of nature softly weaves.
Invoking peace, a harmony profound,
In this sacred space, serenity is found.

So venture forth where the world fades away,
And join the chants of night, come what may.
In the hidden hollow, let your spirit roam,
For in its whispers, every heart finds home.

Serene Melodies Beneath Moonlit Canopies

In shadows deep, where whispers play,
The moonlight weaves a silver ray.
Each note a sigh, a soft caress,
In nature's hush, we find our rest.

The leaves, they dance, a gentle sway,
As night unfolds its velvet stay.
Crickets sing in harmony,
A serenade of reverie.

Beneath the oaks, an echo glows,
Where fireflies flicker, softly close.
The world slows down, a tranquil thread,
In quietude, our dreams are fed.

Stars twinkle bright, a guiding flame,
Each shimmering spark knows our name.
With every breath, the magic grows,
In moonlit grace, our spirit flows.

So linger here, where peace aligns,
In melodies where starlight shines.
Embrace the night, its tender call,
For beneath its glow, we are all whole.

Gentle Songs of the Woodland Heart

Among the trees, the soft winds weave,
A melody that bids us leave.
To wander far in whispered dreams,
Where every glance a secret gleams.

The brook hums low, a lilting tune,
Beneath the watchful eye of moon.
As shadows stretch and night unfurls,
Each sound enchants, the magic swirls.

With every footfall, secrets share,
An ancient rhythm fills the air.
The rustling leaves, a quiet choir,
Awakens hearts and fuels desire.

A fox darts quick with eyes aglow,
While mossy paths invite us slow.
In every breath, the forest sings,
Of earthly truths and wondrous things.

So pause and listen to the night,
Where nature's heart beats pure and bright.
In woodland arms, we find our home,
Together bound, we'll never roam.

The Harmony of Starlit Blooms

In twilight's grace, the blossoms gleam,
Each petal tender, soft as cream.
They sway in sync with evening's song,
Where every moment feels so long.

The garden breathes a whispered thought,
In fragrant hues, our spirits caught.
A symphony of colors bright,
Unfolds beneath the cloak of night.

The moon hangs low, a glowing guide,
As dreams of wanton flowers glide.
With gentle touch, the breezes play,
Awakening joy in dusk's ballet.

Each star above, a silent friend,
In their embrace, our worries mend.
For in the night, the blooms unite,
A tapestry of pure delight.

So let us dance where shadows soar,
On starlit paths, forevermore.
A harmony of hearts entwined,
In nature's song, we shall be blind.

Claybound Symphony at Dusk

In claybound caves, where echoes dwell,
The dusk unveils its secret spell.
With shadows deep and stories long,
The earth hums low a timeless song.

Each winding path, a tale to tell,
Of whispered dreams and ancient well.
The twilight paints the sky in gold,
As night prepares its cloak of bold.

With every footstep, silence grows,
Beneath our feet, the soft earth glows.
A requiem of windswept grace,
Embracing all in warm embrace.

The stars emerge, a twinkling choir,
Each note a spark of cosmic fire.
We gather here, where hearts align,
In nature's song, we intertwine.

So let us linger, hand in hand,
Beside the clay, we make our stand.
With every breath, the night reveals,
A symphony that time conceals.

Harmonizing with the Whispers of Nature

In the forest, secrets weave,
Among the leaves, the whispers cleave.
Gentle winds through branches play,
Nature's voice, a soft ballet.

Sunlight dances on the stream,
Golden sparkles, like a dream.
Birds in chorus sing on high,
Underneath the endless sky.

The petals blush with morning dew,
Colors vibrant, fresh and true.
Butterflies flutter, grace untold,
In this world, magic unfolds.

Mountains stand with stoic pride,
Guardians of the lands they guide.
With each step, a tale retold,
In their shadows, dreams enfold.

Stars emerge as twilight glows,
Whispers linger where night flows.
Tales of old in moonlit beams,
Nature's heart, a world of dreams.

Serenity at the Edge of Enchantment

In the glen where shadows meet,
Winds of calm, a lullaby sweet.
Mist wraps round like a warm embrace,
Time slows here, in this sacred place.

Crickets sing to the fading light,
As day melts into the velvet night.
The brook murmurs its ancient song,
Echoing where the heart belongs.

Stars awaken, one by one,
Guiding wishes, dreams begun.
Silver moonlight on the lake,
Reflecting whispers as they wake.

Gathered stones tell of ages past,
Stories woven, shadows cast.
Each breath taken, pure delight,
An enchantment, serene and bright.

Time stands still in this embrace,
Nature's gifts, a sacred space.
With each heartbeat, the magic flows,
In this haven, my spirit knows.

A Mosaic of Echoes in Magical Realms

In hidden glades, where secrets lie,
Echoes dance beneath the sky.
Fragments of laughter, whispers low,
In this realm where wonders grow.

The trees stand tall with stories old,
Crafting dreams in shades of gold.
Each rustle of leaves a note played,
In nature's orchestra, unafraid.

Moonlit paths invite the brave,
Through enchanted woods, the heart will crave.
Each shadow holds a spark of light,
Guiding lost souls through the night.

Crystalline streams reflect the stars,
Wishing wells and ancient jars.
With each ripple, time suspended,
In this magic, hearts are mended.

Whirls of color, a painter's dream,
In every corner, magic teems.
This mosaic of echoes, vast and grand,
Cradles the dreams of every land.

Velvet Hues in a Canvas of Light

A canvas spread in dawn's embrace,
Velvet hues in a soft space.
The sun dips low, a painter's brush,
Colors blend in a vibrant hush.

Crimson blooms where shadows play,
Whispers of twilight chase the day.
Beneath the boughs, the whispering trees,
Rustling gently in the evening breeze.

Golden rays on grass recline,
Nature's palette, bold, divine.
Every petal, every hue,
Speaks of magic, fresh and new.

Stars ignite in the twilight's glow,
Lighting paths where dreamers go.
A tapestry of light and shade,
In this world where dreams are laid.

In every color, stories wake,
Moments cherished, hearts will take.
A canvas woven, rich and bright,
In velvet hues, we find our light.

The Velvet Touch of Gossamer Nights

In the stillness where shadows glide,
The moon whispers secrets, soft and wide.
Stars twinkle like diamonds, bright and rare,
Draping dreams like silk in the evening air.

Gentle breezes weave through the trees,
Carrying echoes of ancient pleas.
The velvet touch of night enfolds,
Embracing hearts with stories untold.

Crickets sing in a lullaby tune,
Harmonizing with the watchful moon.
Each note a wish born into flight,
Through the velvet touch of gossamer night.

Fingers of mist brush the soft ground,
Revealing wonders that weave around.
In twilight's grasp, magic takes flight,
Spinning tales in the soft, dim light.

As dreams unfurl in a silken dance,
The world slumbers, lost in the trance.
With every heartbeat, the night ignites,
The velvet touch of gossamer nights.

Cradle of Wishes in Hidden Nooks

Amidst the ferns where shadows dwell,
A cradle of wishes weaves its spell.
In hidden nooks, where wildflowers lean,
The heart finds peace in the spaces between.

Petals whisper secrets of the day,
Carried on breezes that softly play.
Each wish a note in nature's song,
Guiding the lost where they belong.

Twinkling fireflies dance in delight,
Casting flickers of magic in the night.
Beneath ancient oaks, the wishes grow,
In the cradle of dreams, there's much to sow.

With every sigh, a heart takes flight,
Chasing the stars, embracing the night.
Hope blooms in the dark, tender and true,
A cradle of wishes awaits me and you.

So venture forth where the wild paths wind,
In hidden nooks, let your heart unwind.
For in the silence, where dreams intertwine,
A cradle of wishes forever will shine.

Soft Footfalls on Gossamer Trails

Through woodlands deep, where silence sleeps,
Soft footfalls tread where the starlight weeps.
Gentle whispers ride the evening breeze,
Leading on paths through the whispering trees.

Silver threads of moonlight gleam,
Guiding the heart on a shimmering dream.
Each step a promise, soft and light,
On gossamer trails that weave through the night.

Angels of twilight guard the way,
In the deepening dusk, where shadows play.
Every rustle, a tale softly spun,
On pathways where earth and sky are one.

With every heartbeat, the magic unfolds,
In the soft embrace of night's gentle holds.
Footfalls like secrets, hush and frail,
Linger in echoes on gossamer trails.

So wander far where the starlight calls,
Embrace the night as the shadow falls.
For in this twilight, you'll find the frail,
Soft footfalls dancing on gossamer trails.

The Dance of Butterflies in Shimmering Light

In gardens lush, where breezes sigh,
Butterflies flit, painting the sky.
Wings of color, graceful and bright,
Join in the dance of shimmering light.

Petals unfurl in a vibrant cheer,
As nature's whispers draw ever near.
Each flutter a heartbeat, soft and free,
In the symphony of life, a melody.

They weave through blooms with elegance rare,
A tapestry woven with delicate care.
In the soft glow of the dawn's embrace,
The dance of butterflies finds its place.

As sunlight cascades in a golden flow,
Each movement tells secrets we long to know.
With every new dawn, they take to flight,
In the dance of butterflies, pure delight.

So let your spirit take wing and soar,
In the gardens where dreams forever adore.
For in that dance, with colors so bright,
Awaits the magic of shimmering light.

Latticework of Faery's Grasp

In twilight's weave, the shadows play,
Where silver lights entwine the day.
A whisper soft, a shimmer bright,
The faeries dance in gentle flight.

Among the glens where secrets gleam,
They curate joy in every dream.
From petals spun with ancient lore,
They beckon hearts to seek for more.

With laughter light as autumn's breeze,
They stir the leaves and bend the trees.
In every corner of the glade,
Their magic stirs, their joys cascade.

Oh, trust the signs that grace your way,
As dusk unfolds the final play.
For in each sigh that drifts between,
The faery's grasp remains unseen.

Whispers of Enchanted Earth

The earth beneath, a sacred hymn,
In rolling hills where shadows swim.
Each blade of grass, a story spun,
Of whispered dreams and laughter's fun.

Beneath the roots where secrets hide,
The echoes of the past abide.
In every stone, in every brook,
The heart of magic waits, unshook.

The sunbeams dance on morning dew,
A canvas bright, a vibrant hue.
And as the soft winds flow and sigh,
The whispers rise to kiss the sky.

Embrace the pulse of silent woods,
The quiet strength of ancient moods.
In every breath that earth imparts,
Lies endless wonder in our hearts.

Soft Echoes of Dreaming Hills

In rolling waves of verdant green,
Echoes soft where dreams convene.
Each hilltop whispers tales untold,
Of bygone times, both brave and bold.

The sunset paints with strokes of gold,
As shadows stretch, a sight to hold.
A gentle breeze, a sighing sound,
Where hope and wonder dance around.

With every step, the path unfolds,
A tapestry of dreams like gold.
Join with the stars, the night so clear,
For in our hearts, all dreams draw near.

So let the echoes guide your way,
Through winding roads where spirits sway.
In whispered tones of twilight thrill,
We find our peace on dreaming hills.

Hues of Twilight in a Petal Rain

The sky ignites with hues so bright,
As day concedes to velvet night.
With petals falling soft like prayer,
The world transforms, a muted flare.

Each color blends, a painter's dream,
Where shadows dance in twilight's gleam.
From crimson blush to azure blue,
The heart awakens, fresh and new.

As evening wraps the world in grace,
The stars emerge to kiss the face.
With every sigh and gentle sigh,
The spirit soars, we learn to fly.

In whispered winds, the stories wane,
While every moment feels the same.
In twilight's soft and swirling rain,
We find our truth, our joy, our pain.

Serenity's Palette in Nature's Embrace

In the hush where shadows play,
The dappled leaves dance and sway,
Beneath the sky, a canvas bright,
Nature's brush strokes shed pure light.

Whispers ride on a gentle breeze,
Among the boughs of ancient trees,
Colors blend, a soft delight,
In every crevice, day turns night.

Rivers hum a soothing tune,
Underneath the silvery moon,
Flowers bloom with fragrant sighs,
A sacred trust in nature lies.

Mountains stand with timeless grace,
Guardians of this tranquil space,
And in their shadow, spirits soar,
Embraced by earth forevermore.

The heartbeat of the world is slow,
In this serene and endless glow,
Each moment rich, a fleeting frame,
In nature's palette, love's true name.

The Sweet Cascade of Celestial Whispers

In twilight's glow where dreams reside,
Celestial whispers softly glide,
Starlight trickles from the skies,
A gentle touch that sweetly ties.

Moonbeams weave through silver trees,
Carrying tales upon the breeze,
Echoes of the night's embrace,
In every heart, a sacred space.

Crickets sing their lullaby,
While shadows flit, the fireflies fly,
A cascade of secrets untold,
In stardust pockets, wonders unfold.

The universe hums a wistful song,
Pulling the dreamers right along,
In radiant pools of cosmic light,
They dance with comets, take their flight.

In each heart, a glimmer shines,
As night adores the world's designs,
With every burst of laughter free,
Celestial whispers call to me.

Pondering at the Edge of Enchanted Dreams

At dawn's edge where fables curl,
Dreamers pause, their minds unfurl,
A tapestry of thoughts in bloom,
Awaiting tales to chase the gloom.

The misty veil begins to lift,
Revealing magic as a gift,
Stories flutter, softly sing,
Every whisper, a new beginning.

With every breath, a wish on air,
Hope and wonder, beyond compare,
Footsteps trace where wishes lay,
In enchanted realms of yesterday.

Fleeting moments, colors blend,
In twilight's grasp, where echoes send,
The heart knows where the wild things play,
In dreams' embrace, they find their way.

Pondering names on a fleeting breeze,
In the fold of time, hearts find ease,
At the edge of dreams, we ride the stream,
Alive and thriving, lost in gleam.

A Curtsy of Light in Mystical Shallows

In stillness deep where waters gleam,
Light performs its graceful theme,
A curtsy of joy, a shimmer bright,
In mystical shallows, pure delight.

Ripples dance on the surface clear,
Echoes of laughter in every sphere,
The sun dips low to kiss the tides,
With secrets that the ocean hides.

Windswept whispers beckon near,
Calling forth the dreams held dear,
With every wave, a story spins,
Awakening all that lies within.

In every splash, a promise swells,
The sea weaves magic with its spells,
Holding footsteps of souls once lost,
In the embrace of ebb and frost.

A symphony of twilight shades,
Amidst the currents, the heart parades,
Each moment cast in liquid light,
In mystical shallows, pure and bright.

Twilight's Embrace on the Faerie Farm

In twilight's glow, the faeries play,
With wings of silk, they dance and sway.
Soft whispers drift through fields of gold,
As secrets of the night unfold.

The twilight wraps the world in dreams,
Where laughter floats on silver beams.
The crops that sway beneath the light,
Are kissed by magic of the night.

Beneath the stars, the fireflies gleam,
In every heart, there's space to dream.
A gentle sigh, the breezes share,
As dusk enfolds the faerie lair.

Among the flowers, shadows hide,
Each petal sighs, a secret guide.
With every blink, the moments freeze,
In twilight's arms, the heart finds ease.

So linger here where faeries dwell,
In dreams that weave a wondrous spell.
For in this farm of twilight's grace,
We find a home in magic's embrace.

The Caress of Petals on the Skin of the Earth

In gardens lush where whispers sigh,
The petals fall as breezes nigh.
Each hue a tale of earth and sun,
In nature's grace, our hearts are one.

The dewdrops cling like diamonds rare,
Caressing blooms with fragrant air.
A tapestry of colors bright,
Awakens dreams in morning light.

With every step on verdant ground,
The silent symphony resounds.
A gentle brush of leaf and blade,
Where all our worries seem to fade.

The earth does hum a soothing tune,
Beneath the warmth of afternoon.
As petals sway in soft delight,
Our spirits soar to newfound heights.

So let us wander hand in hand,
Through gardens strange and wild and grand.
For in this realm of purest mirth,
We feel the caress of the earth.

A Delicate Reverie of Shimmering Dew

With morning's light, a stillness gleams,
Upon the leaves, the dewbeam dreams.
Each drop a world, a whispered prayer,
In nature's heartbeat, pure and rare.

As shadows stretch with gentle grace,
The sun bestows its warm embrace.
In every glimmer, secrets show,
A delicate dance of ebb and flow.

Through fields adorned with sparkling light,
The silver droplets take their flight.
They weave a tale of fleeting time,
A shimmering verse, a gentle rhyme.

And in this moment, pause to see,
The beauty held in fragility.
In dewy whispers, dreams take flight,
A reverie of morning's light.

So chase the dawn, with heart so true,
And find the magic found in dew.
For in each drop, a spark, a sigh,
Awaits the dreamers passing by.

Wisps of Time on Sundrenched Shores

On sundrenched shores where shadows cast,
The whispers of the waves flow fast.
Each footstep soft in golden sand,
Unfolds the stories of the land.

The ocean's song, a lullaby,
Calls out to hearts that wish to fly.
With every tide that sweeps the strand,
A wisp of time slips through our hands.

In salty air, the moments blend,
As sea and sky begin to mend.
The sun dips low, the colors flare,
With painted skies that dance in prayer.

So let us breathe the ocean's tale,
With every wave, our spirits sail.
In harmony with nature's roar,
We find the peace we seek on shore.

For in the twilight, as day departs,
A tapestry weaves in our hearts.
So cherish now the sands we roam,
For wisps of time lead us back home.

Enchantment of the Gentle Stream

In twilight's glow, the stream does sing,
A melody of life in every ring.
Soft whispers dance on sapphire blue,
Embracing secrets known to few.

With pebbles bright, the light does play,
Rippling tales of yesterday.
Within the currents, dreams take flight,
A world concealed from prying sight.

The willows sway, their branches low,
Casting shadows in the flow.
Each shimmering wave, a story spun,
Of moonlit nights and morning sun.

Beneath the arches, fairies prance,
In spirited glee, they twirl and dance.
The gentle breeze, a lover's sigh,
Cradles their laughter as they fly.

So linger here, with heart agleam,
In the enchantment of the stream.
For magic lies in every part,
A soothing balm for the weary heart.

Harmonies in the Whispering Grove

Amidst the trees, a symphony plays,
Each note entwined in the summer's haze.
Leaves converse in a rustling tune,
Beneath the watchful eye of the moon.

Birdsong weaves through the dappled light,
A serenade of day and night.
Branches sway, a gentle ballet,
Celebrating dusk, inviting day.

In emerald depths where shadows wane,
The heart discovers its hidden vein.
Every breath is a whispered prayer,
To the spirits resting without a care.

Flowers nod in the evening's grace,
As twilight blushes on their face.
In the grove, where whispers blend,
Nature's symphony will never end.

So wander slow, let the music call,
In this enchanted grove, you'll find it all.
Harmony wraps around the soul,
A sanctuary where hearts are whole.

Clay Dreams of the Verdant Realm

In fields of green, the dreams take shape,
Crafted by hands, the heart's escape.
Molded by time, and sunlit grace,
In nature's heart, each form finds place.

The potter's wheel spins tales of earth,
Each vessel hums of joy and mirth.
Clay beneath fingers, soft and warm,
A canvas where wild thoughts can swarm.

With every stroke, a story beckons,
From ancient roots where magic reckons.
Winding paths of thought entwine,
In spiral dreams, a flicker divine.

As twilight falls on the verdant land,
Magic swirls in the sculptor's hand.
Nature's art in a crafted frame,
Echoes of life in its silent claim.

So breathe it in, this world so vast,
In clay, the whispers of the past.
The verdant realm holds dreams untold,
In every curve, a heartbeat bold.

Murmurs of the Fae Beneath the Boughs

Beneath the boughs of ancient trees,
The fae convene on twilight's breeze.
With silken wings, they flit and gleam,
Woven closely into nature's dream.

Their laughter tinkles like a chime,
In perfect sync with flowing rhyme.
Among the ferns, they weave their spark,
Igniting magic, though it is dark.

They whisper secrets of moonlit nights,
Of starry skies and wondrous sights.
With every flutter, stories spill,
In enchanted woods, where time stands still.

In hidden glades, the shadows sway,
As fae rejoicing at break of day.
Their gentle giggles, a sweet refrain,
Echo through branches, soft as rain.

So heed the murmurs in the glade,
Where fae and dreams collectively wade.
For in their laughter lies the magic,
A world anew, forever tragic.

Charms of the Woodland Hideaway

In the glade where the soft winds sigh,
Whispers of magic weave and fly.
Dew-kissed leaves in gentle dance,
Guard secrets that hold a fleeting glance.

Beneath the boughs where fairies play,
Time slips like sand, then fades away.
A glimmer here, a shimmer there,
Nature's wonders beyond compare.

Crystal streams sing songs of old,
Stories of warmth in the winter's cold.
In twilight's embrace the owls convene,
Guardians of realms both bright and serene.

Each nook and cranny, a tale to tell,
Of woodland spells where ancients dwell.
My heart finds solace in shadows cast,
In the woodland hideaway, a refuge vast.

Where echoes linger and laughter weaves,
Amidst the silence, the heart believes.
A charm of whispers in the leafy deep,
In this enchanted grove, my soul shall keep.

Lilting Breezes Upon Dreamstone Paths

Through the mist where the lilies bloom,
Whispers ride on the delicate plume.
Moonlight dances on edges fair,
Guiding lost souls through silver air.

Step lightly now on the dreamstone way,
Where shadows play by the dawn's soft ray.
Each sigh of wind carries tales unspoken,
Of wishes made and hearts once broken.

Daisies twirl in their jubilant grace,
Time stands still in this sacred place.
Joy and sorrow weave hand in hand,
As hope begins to softly stand.

Hummingbirds flit, a flash of light,
In the arms of twilight's gentle flight.
Every moment a gem, a fleeting spark,
As dreams ignite in the velvet dark.

Wrapping each traveler's heart so dear,
In gardens alive, with love sincere.
Lilting breezes, a soft embrace,
Along dreamstone paths, a blessed space.

Swaying Shadows of the Enchanted

In the twilight glow where shadows weave,
Mystic stories the stars conceive.
Beneath the arches of ancient trees,
The whispers linger upon the breeze.

A tapestry of light in dusky hues,
Tales of magic in the evening blues.
Swaying shadows, a gentle delight,
Guide the way through the gathering night.

Flickering lanterns in the glen,
Echo the laughter of long-lost friends.
Their joyful cries, a melody sweet,
In the dance of the forest, life feels complete.

The secrets spin in the soft moonlight,
Emboldening spirits, set for flight.
Each heartbeat echoes the forest's song,
In a world where we all belong.

Look closely now, for you might see,
The magic that binds you and me.
Swaying shadows of a night divine,
In the enchanted woods, our souls entwine.

Echoes of a Secret Reverie

In a realm where dreams dare to tread,
Softly whispers fill the quiet thread.
Echoes dance in the moonlit haze,
Where wishes linger in woven ways.

Hidden paths through a tapestry bright,
Guide the wanderers, lost in the night.
With every footfall, a spell is cast,
Unraveling fables from futures past.

Muffled laughter, the nightingale's song,
A serenade where memories belong.
In murmurs of twilight, hearts intertwine,
In secret reveries, pure and divine.

Glimmers of stardust in the deep sky,
Call to the dreamers who soar and fly.
Each heartbeat a rhythm, each breath a chance,
To taste the magic in life's grand dance.

In this hushed symphony, we find our place,
Embraced by the night, our spirits embrace.
Echoes of a secret, a sweet lullaby,
In the heart of the night, we learn to fly.

Caressing the Spirit of the Glade

In the hush of whispering leaves,
A dance of shadows weaves,
Soft sighs of the ancient trees,
Embrace the heart with ease.

Moonlight spills like silver dew,
Kisses petals that gently strew,
With every breath, the magic blooms,
In this glade where desire looms.

The spirit sways in evening's glow,
Where secrets linger, low and slow,
With each twinkle, the night's embrace,
Awakens dreams in hidden space.

Crickets sing their lullabies,
Underneath the starry skies,
Where time is but a fleeting thread,
We find the words left unsaid.

In this realm, the heart takes flight,
Guided by the softest light,
Caressing wonder, gentle, bright,
In the spirit's cherished night.

Galaxies Hiding in Petal Dreams

Petals folded, whispers near,
Softly dreaming in the sphere,
A world where galaxies unfold,
In hues of violet and gold.

Every bloom a cosmic wish,
In the silence, lovers' bliss,
Hope and wonder twirl and spin,
As the night begins to grin.

Stars alight on fragrant air,
Sowing secrets, bright and rare,
Crafting tales in fragrant bliss,
In gardens kissed by starlight's kiss.

Find the cosmos in each sigh,
In the glimmer of the eye,
For within these petals lie,
Whispers of a soft goodbye.

In this dream, we drift and sway,
Through the softest hues of gray,
Galaxies in petals glean,
A tapestry of what has been.

Twilight Serenity of the Gossamer Realm

In twilight's embrace, the shadows twine,
Where whispers of magic softly align,
Gossamer threads spin tales anew,
In a realm adorned with morning dew.

Silken fog wraps the world in bliss,
As twilight paints with a tender kiss,
Each breath a secret, sweet and fair,
In the silence, we find our share.

The stars awaken, shyly peeking,
In the realm where silence is speaking,
A gentle touch from the night so keen,
Guiding hearts through the in-between.

Wings of dreams flutter overhead,
Where brighter futures softly tread,
In whispers of the growing night,
We chase the shadows, pure and light.

In the gossamer realm, we find our place,
A symphony spun in twilight's grace,
Serenity wrapped in the evening's veil,
Where every heartbeat tells a tale.

Fables Carved in the Softest Clay

Once upon a whisper's breath,
Stories crave life, dance with death,
Carved in clay, where dreams reside,
Fables bloom, with hope as guide.

Soft and tender, hands create,
Visions formed from love and fate,
Each curve a journey, proud and true,
In the warmth of the artist's view.

Legends rise with every touch,
Kneaded life that means so much,
In the stillness, wisdom flows,
Through the tales the heart bestows.

Voices echo in the night,
Softly bringing myths to light,
With each breath, a story shared,
In every soul, a dream ensnared.

Fables fashioned, tender clay,
Crafting joys that will not stray,
In these hands, the world we mold,
Holding futures yet untold.

Lullabies from the Glimmering Grotto

In twilight's hush, the waters sing,
With silver notes that softly cling.
A gentle breeze, a whispered tune,
As dreams dance 'neath the watchful moon.

The stones, they sparkle, secrets kept,
Where ancient magic softly wept.
Each ebbing wave, a lullaby,
To calm the restless, loitering sigh.

Among the ferns, a twilight glow,
Where nymphs and sprites in shadows flow.
Their laughter spins like threads of gold,
A tale forgotten, yet retold.

With every note, the night unfolds,
A story woven, brave and bold.
In every heart, a spark ignites,
As lullabies take flight on nights.

And here beneath the starlit skies,
Where moonbeams weave and magic lies,
The grotto stirs, a sacred space,
Where time meets dreams in soft embrace.

Echos from the Lore of Yesterday's Woods

Beneath the boughs where shadows play,
Old whispers weave through night and day.
Each rustling leaf, a tale unfolds,
Of knights and dames, of ancient gold.

The owls, they call with knowing grace,
In every sound, a memory's trace.
As moonlit paths, they twist and bend,
Inviting wanderers to ascend.

In every nook, the secrets lie,
Of wizards' spells and dreams awry.
The brook's soft babble forms a rhyme,
As echoes drift through threads of time.

With every step, the woods may hum,
In time with heartbeats, steady drum.
A dance with shadows, soft and shy,
Where history lives, yet will not die.

So linger long where legends tread,
And let the tales embrace your head.
For yesterday's woods hold magic true,
In every sigh, a dream anew.

The Glow of Secrets in the Shaded Grove

In the shaded grove where whispers blend,
A light breaks forth, a soft descend.
With dapples bright on mossy beds,
The secrets sleep where silence treads.

Each shadow holds a tale untold,
Of scavenger hunts and treasures old.
Where fairies flit through twilight's lace,
In laughter's echo and playful grace.

With every breeze, the branches sway,
Carrying thoughts that drift away.
A circle forms, a spell in air,
With magic woven everywhere.

Here time stands still, with glowing cheeks,
Where nature speaks in mystic peaks.
The heart finds comfort, hope, and joy,
In every glimmer, every ploy.

So wander slow, enjoy the pace,
Embrace the light, the soft embrace.
For in this grove, the secrets lie,
In every beam that wanders by.

Faerie Glimmers of Distant Dawn

As dawn peeks shyly past the night,
A faerie dance brings forth the light.
With glimmers bright on dewy leaves,
The world awakens, gently weaves.

In pastel hues, the sky unfurls,
While morning sings and magic twirls.
From petals soft, the fragrance spills,
As sunlight kisses hidden hills.

With every ray, hope flickers free,
A promise wrapped in mystery.
The dawn ignites what shadows bore,
A new beginning, evermore.

As faerie whispers chase the night,
In golden dawn, the heart takes flight.
Each sparkle shows a path unknown,
With faerie secrets humbly sown.

So cherish each soft golden glow,
Embrace the magic, let it flow.
For in the dawn, life starts afresh,
With faerie glimmers, hearts enmesh.

Secrets Carved in Faerie Silhouettes

In twilight's grasp, where shadows dance,
The faeries weave their secret trance.
With whispers soft, they light the night,
Carving dreams in silver light.

Underneath the ancient oak,
A breath of magic, softly spoke.
Tales of old, in glimmers bright,
Entwined in love, a wondrous sight.

Where moonbeams twirl in playful glee,
The heart unlocks what's yet to be.
With each soft sigh, the stars align,
As faerie magic wraps, entwine.

Through glades of green, they prance and play,
In shimmering hues, their spirits sway.
In every corner, secrets glide,
Forever held, where dreams abide.

So listen well to evening's call,
For faerie whispers beckon all.
Their stories rest on fragile wings,
In twilight's realm, where wonder springs.

Tender Rhythms of the Mossy Glade

Beneath the boughs where shadows blend,
The forest sings, a whispered friend.
Mossy carpets, a soft embrace,
In nature's arms, we find our place.

With every breath, the world unwinds,
In gentle hues, the heart unbinds.
The brook's sweet laugh, a lullaby,
With sighs of leaves as breezes sigh.

The dance of light through branches weave,
A fleeting glance, a web beleaves.
Where solitude meets love's own grace,
In quiet glades, we find our space.

While ferns unfold, the heart ignites,
In tender notes of forest rites.
Each step is guided by the lore,
Of mossy trails that want us more.

So linger long in twilight's fold,
Where stories of the earth are told.
In every whisper, every shade,
Resides the love, the mossy glade.

Echoes of Serenity in the Heart of Nature

In nature's arms, a soft refrain,
The whispers of the wild take gain.
Here echoes bloom, as silence sings,
In every nook, a peace it brings.

The rustle of the leaves above,
A symphony of light and love.
With every breeze, a portrait drawn,
Of tranquil grace at break of dawn.

The gentle flow of a stream's caress,
Harmonies of heart, we must confess.
Among the trees, serenity thrives,
In living songs, the heart derives.

Where petals float on morning mist,
In nature's breath, we find our bliss.
The world slows down in golden rays,
Our souls entwined in quiet stays.

So wander forth in boundless peace,
Where echoes find their sweet release.
In the heart of nature's gentle sway,
We find the light of every day.

Celandine Cascades of Whispering Winds

In sunlit fields where shadows play,
Celandines dance, a bright display.
The whispering winds, they tell a tale,
Of wandering paths and gentle gale.

Through valleys rich with colors bright,
Each flower sways, a pure delight.
The breeze, it brushes through the green,
A fleeting glance of worlds unseen.

The golden petals, soft and fair,
Sing of secrets carried in air.
With every sigh, a story weaves,
Of whispered dreams in dappled leaves.

As twilight falls, the colors gleam,
Beneath the moon, the flowers dream.
With silver threads, the night descends,
In every breath, the heart transcends.

So let the winds, like poems, flow,
In nature's hand, our spirits grow.
With celandine's glow, the world is spun,
A waltz of life, forever begun.

The Allure of Fable and Fantasy

In realms where dreams are spun in gold,
A tale of old, forever told.
With dragons bold and wizards wise,
Adventure waits beneath the skies.

The whispers dance on twilight air,
Each secret felt, each heart laid bare.
With every stir, the stories rise,
Enchanting echoes, timeless ties.

In shadowed woods where fairies play,
The magic lingers, night and day.
With starlit paths, the brave explore,
A hidden world, forevermore.

Through mist and moonlight, dreams unfold,
A tapestry of fables bold.
Where every heart can find its home,
In lands of wonder, we may roam.

So grasp the quill, let ink take flight,
For magic lives in words we write.
A journey starts with every page,
In whispered tales, we find our sage.

Beneath the Canopy of Timeless Whispers

Beneath the leaves where shadows play,
The ancient trees hold stories' sway.
With every breeze, a tale takes flight,
In whispered words, both soft and light.

The brook hums low a gentle tune,
Reflecting stars and silver moon.
In nature's heart, the secrets blend,
As day meets night, and dreams ascend.

Each root entwines with memories old,
Of lovers lost and legends bold.
The whispering winds, a sacred sound,
Through timeless woods, adventure found.

In every rustle, a promise spun,
Of battles fought and victories won.
The canopy, a living shroud,
Where hopes take flight, and fears are cowed.

So linger here, let time stand still,
And feel the pulse of nature's will.
For in the silence, treasures gleam,
Beneath the canopy, we dream.

Chants of the Wind Through Woven Branches

Amid the forest, the breezes sing,
Of forgotten tales and endless spring.
Each note a shimmer, a lullaby,
As branches sway beneath the sky.

The echoes weave through every hue,
With whispered secrets meant for few.
They beckon forth both hearts and minds,
In nature's arms, true magic finds.

As twilight settles, shadows blend,
The wind does dance, a faithful friend.
With every gust, the stories trace,
A tapestry of time and space.

From ancient roots to towering boughs,
The forest sways, the spirit bows.
In every rustle, hope reclaims,
The chants of life, in soft refrains.

So close your eyes and lose your way,
Let whispered winds your heart betray.
For in their arms, we learn to see,
The woven song of destiny.

Magic Weaved in a Tapestry of Colors

In every hue, a story's spun,
A canvas bright, where dreams are won.
With strokes of gold and shades of blue,
The magic dances, bold and true.

The sunset paints the sky with flair,
A masterpiece beyond compare.
With every dusk, new wonders blaze,
In colors rich, the heart obeys.

A garden blooms with every shade,
Where visions form and hopes cascade.
In petals soft and leaves so bright,
The music swells in pure delight.

In rivers deep and mountains high,
A palette formed by earth and sky.
Each moment captured, time stands still,
A vibrant world shaped by the will.

So paint your dreams with colors bold,
For life itself is a tale retold.
With every brushstroke, find your part,
In this tapestry, weave your heart.

Whispers of Enchanted Dust

In twilight's glow, the whispers weave,
Of secrets spun, in webs they cleave.
Dancing lights in the muted air,
Cradled dreams, with tender care.

Stars above like lanterns bright,
Guide our hearts through the gentle night.
With every sigh, the magic swells,
In hushed tones, the universe tells.

Hidden paths of shimmering grace,
Find your solace in this embrace.
Every rustle, a story unfolds,
As enchanted dust, in silence, molds.

Lullabies in Moonlit Gardens

In gardens kissed by silver light,
Where shadows dance and hearts take flight.
The moon hums soft, a lullaby sweet,
Crickets play on the cool grass seat.

Petals unfurl, in whispers they sigh,
While fireflies twinkle, as night drifts by.
A breeze carries secrets, old and wise,
Beneath the watchful, starlit skies.

In this haven, the world fades slow,
Only dreams and starlight glow.
Each moment spun in twilight's grace,
In moonlit gardens, find your place.

Echoes of Enigma and Earth

In the forest deep, echoes arise,
Where mystery lurks beneath lush skies.
Roots beneath, with stories entwined,
Echoes of enigma, lovingly mined.

Mountains stand firm, like ancient guards,
Witness to tales written in stars.
The wind carries whispers from the past,
A timeless song, steadfast and vast.

Footsteps on paths where shadows play,
Guide us to realms where secrets lay.
With every heartbeat, the earth will share,
Echoes of life, a wondrous affair.

Secrets of the Gossamer Realm

Beyond the veil, in a realm so fair,
Dance the secrets in the cool night air.
Gossamer threads of dreams untold,
Weave a tapestry of wonders bold.

With every flutter, a story spins,
Of lost beginnings and quiet wins.
Where time stands still, and wishes gleam,
In this hidden place, we softly dream.

A flicker, a sigh, in shadows cast,
Hold the key to futures vast.
In the gossamer realm, hearts combine,
Secrets of magic, forever entwined.

Melodies of the Verdant Veil

In the hush of twilight's glow,
Where whispers of green gently flow,
The leaves weave secrets on the air,
Enchanting hearts in beauty rare.

A songbird strums a soft refrain,
As sunlight dances on the lane,
With every note, the forest sighs,
A harmony that never dies.

Beneath the boughs of ancient trees,
The melodies stir like a breeze,
Each rustling leaf a tale to tell,
In this enchanted, verdant swell.

The brook joins in, with laughter clear,
A lullaby that draws you near,
As shadows stretch and day abates,
The magic of the night awaits.

So linger here, beneath the shade,
Where nature's symphony is made,
In melodies so pure and bright,
That linger on the edge of night.

Cradle of the Spirit's Wandering

Upon the hills where wildflowers bloom,
A spirit wanders, free of gloom,
In every petal, color, and scent,
A journey of the heart is meant.

Through valleys deep and rivers wide,
The spirit travels, full of pride,
With every step, a story grows,
In whispers of the wind that blows.

The sun bestows a gentle kiss,
On meadows wrapped in nature's bliss,
Where echoes of laughter fill the air,
Reminding all who wander there.

In twilight's hush, the stars ignite,
Guiding the spirit through the night,
A cradle made of dreams and lore,
Where every heartbeat seeks for more.

So follow where the wild things lead,
Embrace the paths that fate will seed,
For in the cradle of the free,
Your spirit finds its destiny.

Voices of the Twilight Bloom

As dusk descends, the petals sigh,
The twilight bloom begins to fly,
With colors blending, soft and bright,
A tapestry of day and night.

A chorus rises from the earth,
In shadows deep, a sacred birth,
The flowers whisper tales of yore,
In languages of love and lore.

The moonlight casts a silver gleam,
Transforming every fragrant dream,
With sighs that ripple through the air,
In every blossom's soft, sweet care.

The stars above, like lanterns set,
Invite the world to not forget,
That voices echo when we listen,
In every bloom, a heart's bright mission.

So let your spirit dance and sway,
With voices of the night at play,
For in the twilight's gentle gloom,
Awakes the magic of the bloom.

Bytes of the Nature's Crescendo

In the tapestry of time and space,
Nature weaves its raw embrace,
With bits and bytes of life's delight,
A crescendo calling through the night.

The rustling leaves in syncopate,
A rhythm only hearts relate,
Each ripple, shout, and subtle pause,
Unfolding nature's sacred laws.

Through mountain peaks and river bends,
The story of the earth transcends,
With every heartbeat, every breeze,
A symphony that aims to please.

So listen closely to the sound,
Where love and life are tightly bound,
For in the bytes of nature's song,
We find the place where we belong.

In harmony, with earth's ascent,
Each moment's fleeting energy spent,
A crescendo builds, a timeless call,
In nature's arms, we rise, we fall.

Harmonies Beneath the Canopy

In the woods where shadows play,
Soft whispers dance with leaves at sway,
A symphony of twinkling light,
Calls forth the magic of the night.

Crickets sing, the fireflies gleam,
Woven threads in a silver dream,
Nature's pulse beneath the trees,
A secret world, a gentle breeze.

Mossy paths with tales to tell,
Of ancient owls and wise old spells,
Every step, a story spun,
In the moonlit glow, we come undone.

With every rustle, hearts take flight,
In the embrace of starry night,
Echoes of laughter weave through air,
In this haven, free from care.

So linger here, where wonders grow,
Where time stands still and souls can flow,
Beneath the canopy, we belong,
In harmony, we sing our song.

Fables in the Gossamer Glow

Once upon a twilight's grace,
Magic spun in a soft embrace,
A tapestry of tales untold,
In glimmers bright, the night unfolds.

Fairies dance on moonlit streams,
Whispers caught in fragile dreams,
Every petal tells a tale,
Of hopes and wishes, love's sweet sail.

Windswept stories twirl and fly,
As the stars paint songs in the sky,
A tapestry where hearts entwine,
In gossamer threads, the fates align.

With every spark, a wish ignites,
Chasing shadows, lighting nights,
In the realm where wishes roam,
There lies a place we call our home.

So gather close, let dreams take flight,
In fables wrapped in radiant light,
For every heartbeat writes a line,
In this sacred space, divine.

Dreams Woven with Starlight

In the quiet hush of twilight's glow,
Dreams are woven like threads of snow,
Each flicker of light a whispered quest,
In the fabric of night, we find our rest.

Amidst the shadows, wishes bloom,
Soft as night with its velvet plume,
Every star a tiny spark,
Illuminating paths, even in dark.

Through the silence, our hearts embrace,
Floating gently in time and space,
The cosmos hums a lullaby,
As twinkling wonders fill the sky.

In this realm of gold and blue,
Where every dream feels fresh and new,
We dance on clouds of pure delight,
In the tapestry of endless night.

So close your eyes and breathe it in,
Let the magic of dreams begin,
For in this space, we come alive,
Woven with starlight, we will thrive.

Murmurs of the Silken Breeze

Softly falls the twilight's sigh,
As shadows breathe and moments fly,
The breeze carries secrets sweet,
Where every heart and memory meet.

Through the trees, a melody sways,
The world transforms in gentle ways,
Whispers weave through the evening air,
A silken touch, a lover's flare.

Songs of old in the rustling grass,
Echo tales that softly pass,
Each note a memory, bright and clear,
Gathered 'neath the moonlight here.

With every gust, a promise made,
In the shadows, dreams invade,
Carried forth on the evening tide,
In the silence where secrets hide.

So listen close, for love is near,
In every sigh, in every tear,
The breeze murmurs soft and low,
A serenade where magic flows.

The Lull of Leaves in an Enchanted Wake

In whispered shades the leaves do sway,
Beneath the moon's soft, silver ray.
A dance of shadows, wild and free,
In dreams entwined, they call to me.

The brook murmurs with gentle might,
As stars awaken in the night.
Their twinkling laughter, sweet and light,
A symphony of pure delight.

Among the trees, the fairies play,
Their laughter brightens dusk till day.
Soft petals drift, a velvet sound,
In twilight's arms, they spin around.

The forest breathes a quiet tune,
Beneath the watchful gaze of moon.
Each branch a verse, each leaf a word,
Their secrets softly, gently stirred.

Rest now, dear heart, let worries cease,
Embrace the night, and find your peace.
For in this hush, a dreamer's way,
Awaits the dawn of another day.

Caressing the Dusk with Fairy Graces

When evening falls, and shadows blend,
The fairies glide, on whispers send.
With silver wings, they weave and dart,
Embracing dusk, they seek the heart.

They twirl on petals, soft and small,
As twilight casts its gentle thrall.
A waltz of colors, bright and rare,
In every breath, a hint of air.

Through ferns and woods, where secrets hide,
Their giggles echo, side by side.
The evening glows with magic's hand,
Illuminating this sweet land.

With tender touch, they brush the ground,
A lullaby in breezes found.
Each star a wish, a hope, a dream,
In dusky realms, all thoughts redeem.

So close your eyes, let stillness reign,
For in this moment, joy remains.
The fairies dance, with light embrace,
Caressing souls with fairy grace.

Gentle Breezes that Kiss the Soul of the Wood

The woodlands sigh with gentle grace,
As breezes whisper, time and place.
Each rustling leaf, a soft refrain,
Invites the heart to dance again.

With every gust, a tale unfolds,
Of ancient trees and secrets old.
The woodland's breath, a sacred song,
In harmony, we all belong.

As dappled sunlight weaves its thread,
The path ahead is gently spread.
Through mossy glades and twilight streams,
In nature's arms, we chase our dreams.

So let the breezes wrap you tight,
In tender folds of soft twilight.
For in these woods, a world of peace,
Awaits the heart, where worries cease.

With every step, find joy anew,
In every breeze, a love so true.
The wood's sweet song will steady you,
A calming balm for spirits blue.

Reverberations of Whimsy Within Nature's Heart

In wooded realms where wild things play,
A world of whimsy lights the way.
With laughter bright, the creatures sing,
Their joy a sweet and wondrous thing.

The brook's soft babble, clear and bright,
Holds echoes of the day's delight.
Each ripple speaks of stories vast,
Of fleeting moments that drift past.

The daisies dance beneath the sun,
Each petal holds the joy of fun.
With every breeze, they nod and sway,
Inviting all to join their play.

As twilight draws its curtain near,
The fireflies burst, a light to cheer.
They flicker dreams, both bold and slight,
Whispering wishes into the night.

Embrace the whimsy, breathe it in,
Let nature's heart ignite within.
For every sound and sight we find,
Holds wonders, timeless and unconfined.

Elysian Murmurs of Fairy Dust

In glades where whispers intertwine,
The breeze weaves tales, both soft and fine.
Tiny lights dance 'neath silvery beams,
Carrying secrets, and children's dreams.

A flutter of wings, so delicate, sweet,
Echoes of laughter in shadows discreet.
Mirth in the murmurs, twilight's embrace,
Magic ignites in this hidden space.

Rustling leaves share the stories they hide,
Of shimmering fairies with wisdom so wide.
Each twinkle a promise, a fleeting delight,
Painting the dusk with ethereal light.

From petals of blossoms, a soft lull is spun,
Threads of enchantment, its journey begun.
In every soft sigh, a tale to be told,
In the heart of the night, with stardust of gold.

Tranquil Breath of the Celestial Grove

Beneath the boughs where the starlight fades,
A river of peace in the twilight cascades.
Each breath a dream, a soft, gentle flow,
In the heart of the grove where the wild creatures go.

Murmurs of nature caress the still air,
Whispers of wisdom float lightly, rare.
Gathering echoes of moments divine,
In the cradle of trees where fairies entwine.

Time drifts like shadows, unhurried and free,
Carving old stories from each sturdy tree.
The night sings a hymn, a calming refrain,
Linking the hearts of the moon and the rain.

Lost in the magic of soft velvet dusk,
Each flower blooms deep, imbued with their trust.
Feel the embrace of the night as it calls,
In the world of the grove, enchantment enthralls.

The Silent Lullaby of Ancient Dreams

In the quiet of night, when shadows play,
Old dreams awaken, drifting away.
The stars hum a tune, gentle and low,
Guiding the souls where the ancients go.

Whispers of time flutter softly about,
A tapestry woven with laughter and doubt.
Each sigh a chapter from ages long past,
A lullaby murmured, eternally cast.

Sleepy-eyed creatures nestle in peace,
Wrapped in the night, where worries cease.
Crickets compose symphonies tranquil and sweet,
Their serenades mingling with heartbeats discreet.

In the arms of the moon, forgotten they drift,
Carried by starlight, their spirits uplift.
Awake in the silence, where dreams intertwine,
In the heart of the night, endless and divine.

Threads of Light in Luminous Twilight

In twilight's embrace, the world gleams bright,
Threads of light weave through shadows of night.
With every heartbeat, a shimmer unfolds,
Stories of warmth in the twilight they hold.

Glistening pathways where wishes take flight,
Carved in the colors of soft, gentle light.
Each moment a jewel, lost in the haze,
Illuminating futures with magical rays.

The sky blushes golden, surrendering stars,
Dancing with whispers of past and of scars.
In the tapestry spun of the evening's sweet breath,
Hope lingers gently, unbroken by death.

The harmony stirs as day meets the night,
Inviting the dreams to take wing in their flight.
Threads of pure wonder, they shimmer and twine,
Luminous whispers, eternally shine.

Conversations with Earth and Ether

Whispers rise from mossy stones,
In the deep embrace of groaning roots.
The earth speaks in gentle tones,
Binding life in unseen pursuits.

Breezes carry ancient lore,
Each leaf a tale of sun and rain.
A language rich, forevermore,
Echoes in the wild terrain.

Stars shimmer in the velvet sky,
Their questions dance on moonlit beams.
The ether sings, and we reply,
Together weaving fragile dreams.

Streams reflect the truths we hold,
In ripples bright, they seem to sigh.
With every current, stories told,
We learn of life, and not to cry.

Thus, in harmony we dwell,
With earth and ether, hand in hand.
In every sigh and song they tell,
A bond that time cannot withstand.

Shadows Dancing in the Fungal Twilight

In twilight's hush, the shadows creep,
Mushrooms sway in dance with night.
Their caps aflame, secrets to keep,
Beneath the stars, they twirl in flight.

Moonlit spores in soft descent,
Glide upon the breath of dreams.
Nature's pulse, a sweet lament,
In silent groves, the magic gleams.

Tails of light brush tender sting,
As tendrils weave a tapestry.
Fungal whispers sharply sing,
Of all that dwells in mystery.

Among the roots, the shadows jive,
With every flicker, tales unfurl.
From dark to light, the spirits thrive,
In the deep woods, they twist and whirl.

Echoes linger, soft and sly,
An ancient force in every sway.
In shadows dancing by and by,
The pulse of nature holds its play.

Embraces of Elysian Synthesis

In galaxies of golden hue,
Where wildflowers kiss the breeze,
Embraces bloom in morning dew,
Each petal begs the heart to seize.

With every breath, a world anew,
A fusion bright of earth and sky.
In harmony, the spirit grew,
As nature's colors flutter by.

The whispers bend, entwined as one,
In every grove where bodies sway.
A symphony, its chords are spun,
In depths where light and shadows play.

From sacred soil, life finds its way,
As roots embrace the promise made.
In vibrant hues, they twist and sway,
A living dance that won't soon fade.

So let us weave with gentle hands,
A tapestry of bright delight.
In Elysium where love expands,
We'll celebrate our joined twilight.

Reflections in the Dappled Glow

In dappled light, we find our names,
Each flicker speaks of who we are.
With golden whispers, life contains,
The warmth that glimmers from afar.

A mirror shines through leafy crowns,
Each shadow threads a path of grace.
Through sylvan realms, where joy abounds,
We dance in time, a sweet embrace.

The sun peeks in, a playful sprite,
Playing hide and seek with dreams.
In every nook, the world ignites,
And nature hums, or so it seems.

Beneath the boughs, our spirits soar,
As laughter mingles with the breeze.
In every heart, a tale of yore,
Is whispered soft among the trees.

So let us wander, hand in hand,
Through dappled paths of forest's flow.
In timeless bonds, we understand,
The beauty held in every glow.

www.ingramcontent.com/pod-product-compliance
Lightning Source LLC
Chambersburg PA
CBHW060336160125
20421CB00003B/49